Money
Saving and Spending

Abigail Richter

Rosen
REAL
READERS

The Rosen Publishing Group, Inc.
New York

Money is the **coins** and **bills** we use to buy things. Each coin or bill stands for a different **amount** of money.

Hundreds of years ago in the United States, people traded things they had, like eggs, for things they needed, like cloth.

The United States started making coins in 1652. People began trading money for the things they needed.

People work to **earn** money.
Some children earn money for
doing work at home.

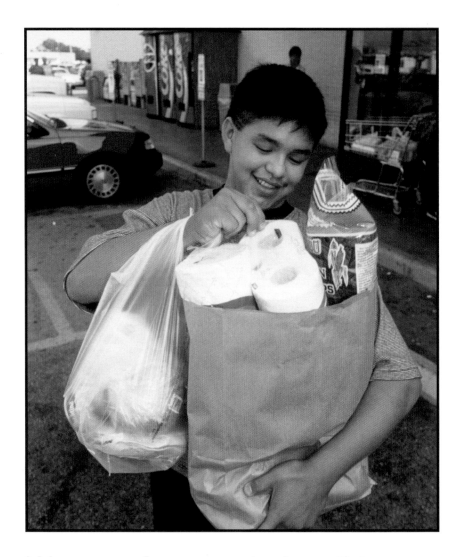

We **spend** money to buy things we need, like food and clothes.

We also spend money to buy things we want, like toys and books.

Sometimes we spend money on small things we want, like popcorn at the movies.

We can also **save** our money to buy big things, like a house or a car.

Many people save their money in a **bank**. A bank is a place where you can safely keep your money.

Sometimes it is better to save your money than to spend it right away. You can save it to buy something special, like a bike!

Glossary

amount The number of things in one group.

bank A place where people keep their money.

bill A piece of paper money.

coin A flat, round piece of metal used as money.

earn To get money for doing work.

save To keep something that you can use later.

spend To trade money for something that you need or want.